I STILL LOVE YOU

~~ UTKARSH PRAKASH ~~

Prologue: The First Glimpse of Love

Love is supposed to bring happiness, they say. For me, it brought happiness, pain, strength, and weakness—all wrapped in the name of Aadya.

I still remember the first time I saw her—how her presence pulled me into a world I didn't know existed. Her eyes had something that held me still, and in that moment, I knew something in me had changed. It was the first glimpse, and I was already gone.

I gave her my heart, without hesitation. My love for her wasn't just a feeling—it became the reason I smiled, the reason I stayed awake at night, the reason I lost parts of myself.

I confessed to her. I poured my soul out, waiting for a word—*yes* or *no*—but she stayed silent. That silence is what holds me today. It's the thread I cling to, the hope I refuse to let go of.

Sometimes she replied, sometimes she didn't. Her seen messages felt like unanswered prayers, and my mind, an overthinker's chaos, made me feel like I'd already lost her. But I tell myself—maybe it's not over. Maybe this is just time testing me.

I am afraid. Afraid of a life without her, afraid of losing something that never truly felt mine, yet always belonged to my heart.

This is not just a story. This is my truth. Aadya, if you ever read this, know that my heart beats your name—broken, but still beating.

This is our story. And I still love you.

Book Content (Table of Contents)

Chapter 1: When Our Eyes Met

They say life changes in moments—quiet, unexpected moments that slip in without warning and leave you different forever. For me, that moment had a name—**Aadya**. I didn't know it then, but when our eyes met for the first time, something inside me shifted, as if my heart had found its rhythm for the first time.

It was an ordinary day, the kind that comes and goes without leaving a trace. I wasn't looking for love. In fact, I wasn't looking for anything. But maybe love has a way of finding you when you least expect it, when your guard is down, and your heart is unprepared. That's how she found me—unprepared, unsuspecting, unaware of the storm she would bring into my life.

I still remember the first glance—her eyes were deep, calm, and unknowingly dangerous. There was a strange kind of peace in her presence, the kind that made the world feel quieter. My eyes caught hers for only a few seconds, but in that short span, my mind painted a thousand possibilities. The noise of the world faded, and all I could focus on was **her**.

I don't know if she noticed me that day. I don't even know if I mattered in that moment to her the way she did to me. But something about her stayed. Her image, her aura, the way she walked like she carried the universe in her eyes—it haunted me, in the most beautiful way possible.

From that day on, everything changed. She wasn't just a girl; she became a thought that wouldn't leave me. Every time I closed my eyes, I saw her smile—soft, warm, and unfamiliar, yet comforting. Every song, every love story I heard suddenly felt personal. Aadya became the poetry my soul didn't know it needed.

At first, all I had was a name — **Sneha**.

That was the name I heard from someone, and for a while, that's what I called her in my mind. I didn't know much about her, but even with just that name, I found myself thinking about her more than I should have. I was curious — not just about who she was, but why she made my heart feel things I couldn't explain. I started noticing the smallest details — the way she laughed with her friends, the way her hair fell gently over her face, the way her presence seemed to light up even the dullest places.

Days passed, and my feelings didn't fade — they grew. Deeper, stronger, uncontrollable. It was like my heart had chosen her before my mind could even understand why.

And then came **June 27, 2024** — a date etched into my memory, not because of anything grand, but because that was the day I learned her real name.

Aadya.

Three syllables that felt like a song. When I heard it for the first time, I don't know why, but something clicked inside me. *Sneha* had been the girl I admired from a distance. But **Aadya**—she became the girl I prayed for. The girl I loved.

It felt like the universe had revealed something sacred to me. Aadya — her name had weight, grace, and a strange sense of destiny tied to it. And after that day, every time I whispered her name to myself, it felt real, like she was a part of me. Not just someone I admired, but someone I *belonged to*, even if she didn't know it.

I started mentioning her in my prayers.

Every night before I closed my eyes, I folded my hands and whispered the same words, *"God, please protect this girl. Keep her happy, keep her safe, and one day, make her mine. I will never let a single scratch touch her. I promise you, I will love her like no one ever could."*

It wasn't just infatuation. It wasn't just a crush. This was something different — purer, deeper, and terrifying. Loving her gave me strength, but it also made me vulnerable. Because the thought of losing her, of never having her, felt like a storm waiting to destroy me.

Yet, I was willing to risk it all. Just for her.

Loving Aadya wasn't easy.

It wasn't the kind of love where you hold hands, exchange sweet words, and share laughter under the stars. No. It was the kind of love where your heart aches in silence, where your soul whispers her name in the dark, and where your eyes well up with tears because you love her so much, but she doesn't even know the depth of it.

There were nights I cried for her.

Not because she hurt me — she never even said a word that could hurt me. But her *silence*—God, her silence—broke me in ways I can't explain. I would send her a message, simple words, nothing heavy, just something to let her know I cared, that I was thinking of her. Sometimes she replied, and in those moments, it felt like the world was right, like my heart could breathe. But then came the days when she left my messages on *seen*. No reply. No words. Just silence.

And that silence screamed louder than any rejection.

Being an overthinker, my mind played with me like a cruel game. *Maybe she doesn't care. Maybe I'm nothing to her. Maybe I already lost her, and I just can't see it.* Thoughts like these consumed me, tearing me apart from the inside. And no matter how much I told myself to stay strong, to have faith, the tears came anyway.

I would stare at my phone screen, hoping, praying for a message — just one message — that would pull me out of this storm. But most times, it never came. And I was left alone with my thoughts, drowning in love that had no place to go.

There were nights I lay awake, staring at the ceiling, tears streaming down my face, clutching my chest as if the pain could be held, as if the emptiness could be filled. I cried not because I was weak, but because loving her made me *feel* so much. She became my everything — my strength, my weakness, my reason to smile, and my reason to cry.

And yet, through all the pain, I never stopped loving her. I *couldn't* stop. Because Aadya wasn't just a girl I loved. She became a part of me — her name etched into every heartbeat, her face in every dream, her voice the echo in my silence.

I begged God, not for riches, not for success — just for her. I told Him, *"Please, don't take her away from me. Let me love her, protect her, make her mine. Let me keep her safe. I don't care if the world turns against me, just let her be with me. I swear, I'll never let a single tear touch her eyes. Let me carry her pain, her sadness, her fears — just let her smile with me."*

But sometimes, it felt like even God was silent.

Still, I loved her. Even when it hurt. Even when the tears wouldn't stop. Even when I felt like I was falling apart. Because somehow, loving

Aadya, even from afar, even in silence, gave my life meaning.

They say love is about presence — being together, sharing moments, holding hands. But what do you do when all you have is *memories* and *pictures*? When the person you love the most feels like a dream you can't touch, a voice you can't hear, a presence you can't feel — yet still, you love them with every fiber of your being?

I had more than **100 photos of Aadya**.
Some were random, some candid, some from the days she smiled without knowing someone was

watching, loving her from a distance. To anyone else, they were just pictures — pixels on a screen. But to me, they were everything. My treasure. My escape. My pain.

I stared at them *more than 100 times a day*.
Sometimes with a soft smile, sometimes with *tears flooding my eyes*, sometimes with a hollow ache in my chest that words could never explain. I would hold my phone like it was her, my eyes locked on her face, and silently, I would *break*. On the outside, I looked fine. But inside, I was crying — loudly, desperately, endlessly.

There were moments I couldn't take it anymore. I'd close my eyes, press my hand to my heart, and *whisper to myself, "She's the only one. The only girl I've ever loved this way, and after her, there will be no one else. No one."*
I meant it.
I still mean it.

I didn't love her to pass time. I didn't love her because I was lonely. I loved her because something about her touched my soul. She became *home*, even if I was just a stranger in hers.

I had **planned my future with her** — not in fantasies, not in dreams, but in pure, real intentions. I imagined waking up next to her, holding her hand through life's storms, building a world where she would feel safe, loved, and cherished every single day. I promised myself that I would protect her smile with my life, that I would never let pain come near her.

I didn't want just moments. I wanted *forever*.
I wanted to see her laugh at silly things, hold her when she cried, celebrate her achievements, and support her through failures. I wanted to grow old with her, watch the stars together, fight, make up,

and live a life built on love, loyalty, and endless care.

My intentions for her were **pure**. Not once did I think of leaving, not once did I imagine anyone else by my side. I only saw *Aadya*.
In my heart, she was — and still is — **the one**.

And even though she didn't know how deeply I loved her, even though her silence sometimes broke me, I held on. Because some loves are not just about being with someone. Some loves are about giving, sacrificing, and waiting — no matter how long, no matter how painful.

I loved Aadya with my whole soul.
And in this lifetime, whether I get
her or not, I know one truth —
I STILL LOVE YOU.

Chapter 2 - Her Smile, My Solace

They say every soul has its solace — something that calms the storms inside, that brings peace even in the darkest hours. For some, it's music. For others, it's silence. But for me, it was **her smile**.

Aadya's smile wasn't just a curve of her lips — it was the only light I needed in my life of chaos. Just one glance at her smile, and everything else faded away — the pain, the overthinking, the fear, the loneliness — all of it. Her smile made the world quiet. It made my heart quiet.

I used to steal glances of her, capturing those fleeting moments in my memory like they were precious treasures. And in every one of those moments, **she was smiling** — unaware that someone's entire universe was held together by that simple expression of joy.

There were days when I felt lost, broken, like I couldn't hold on any longer. But then, I would see her smile — maybe in a photo, maybe in real life — and suddenly, I had the strength to breathe again. Her smile didn't just bring me peace — **it gave me life**.

I remember sitting alone, staring at her photos, my eyes filled with tears, but my lips silently whispering, "*Please God, let this girl always smile like this. Keep her happy. Even if I'm not the reason, just let her keep smiling.*"

Because her smile was **my solace**, my reason, my everything.

I used to wonder — does she know what her smile does to me?

Does she know that whenever her lips curved into that soft, beautiful expression, it felt like someone stitched my broken heart back together, even if just for a moment? Does she know that her smile could stop my tears mid-fall, could pull me out of the darkest thoughts, could make me forget the heaviness I carried inside?

I don't think she knows.
She probably never will.
But I know. I *feel* it. Every single time.

There were moments when I was drowning in overthinking, convinced that I had already lost her, that I never even stood a chance. My mind would spiral — *What if she never feels the same? What if I'm just a face in the crowd to her? What if she leaves?* But then, I'd look at her picture — at

her smile — and suddenly, the chaos would quiet down.

I had **more than 100 photos of her** — each one more precious than gold, each one carrying a piece of my soul. And I would **stare at them again and again**, sometimes more than a hundred times a day. Not because I had nothing better to do, but because her smile was the only thing that gave me peace.

And every time I looked at those photos, tears filled my eyes.
Not just because I missed her, or because I feared losing her — but because **I loved her that deeply**, that truly. And the only thing I ever wanted from God was to see her

smile, always. Even if I wasn't the reason behind it. Even if I never got to hold her hand. Even if I cried alone while watching her live her life.

I whispered to myself, over and over again, "*She is the only one I love, the only one I will ever love. After her, there is no one. No one.*" And I meant every word. Because my love for Aadya wasn't just about wanting to be with her — it was about **protecting her happiness**, about cherishing her smile, about keeping her safe from the world, even if I stood in the shadows.

I had planned a future with her —
a pure future, built on love,
respect, care. I imagined waking up
next to that smile, falling asleep
with it, and living every single day
just to protect it. I promised myself
that I would never let any harm
come to her, that I would shield
her from every sadness, every fear,
every scar.

Her smile was **my solace**.
And I would give up everything —
everything — just to keep it alive.

Chapter 3 – The Days I lived for her

There's a difference between living and existing.
Before her, I was just… *existing*.
Breathing, moving, surviving. But when Aadya entered my life — everything changed. Suddenly, I wasn't just passing time. **I was living. For her.**

Every morning, my first thought was **her**.
Every night, my last prayer was **her name**.
In between, it was all **her smile**, **her voice**, **her memory**.

I didn't need a reason to think of her — **she was my reason**. The reason I smiled. The reason I kept going, even on the days I was breaking inside. I didn't care if the world understood. I didn't care if anyone knew. Because for me, **loving Aadya became life itself**.

There were days when I'd stare at my phone, waiting for a message from her. Just a *"Hi"* could light up my whole day. And if it didn't come, I'd still wait — because **I was living for her**, not for myself.

I would go through my day, doing things for the sake of it, but inside, I was constantly *thinking of her*. Wondering where she was, if she was okay, if she was smiling. And every time my mind drifted to her — which was *always* — my heart ached, not because I didn't love her, but because **I loved her too much.**

I lived **for her texts**, even when they came after hours...
I lived **for her photos**, which I'd stare at until my eyes filled with tears...
I lived **for her happiness**, even when it didn't include me...
I lived **for her silence**, trying to find meaning in the emptiness...

Every beat of my heart, every breath I took — was tied to **her existence**.

And no matter how much I cried, how broken I felt, how lonely those days were — I never stopped. I couldn't. Because **she became my world**, and I was living *for her*, not *with her*, and that made all the difference.

27th February, 2025 — the day I gathered all the courage I had, every broken piece of myself, and **confessed my love** to Aadya.

I thought my heart couldn't take any more pain than I had already endured in silence. But that day... I realized I was wrong. *So wrong.*

I told her everything. My feelings. My fears. My dreams — all wrapped in her. I poured my soul out to her, hoping she'd see just how much I loved her — how deeply, how truly. I wasn't expecting magic, I wasn't asking for the world — just a sign, a **little hope**.

And yet... when I asked her, in the most vulnerable tone I've ever used, "*Will I ever make you mine?*" — her reply crushed me.

She didn't say *yes*.
She didn't say *no*.
She simply said, "**I don't know... maybe you can become successful.**"

Success? My love wasn't built on success. It wasn't measured by money or fame. My love was **pure**, **selfless**, **real**. But in that moment, it felt like my love was weighed against *something I couldn't control*.

Her words... they haunt me. Every day. Every night.
From that day — **27th February** — my pain became heavier.
Because now, I wasn't just loving her... I was **hurting for her**.

That one sentence — "maybe you can become successful" — it replayed in my mind like a broken record.
Was I not enough now? Would

success make me worthy?
My heart whispered, *You love her with your soul, isn't that enough?*
But her words echoed louder.

Since that day, every time I looked at her photos — the 100+ images I kept like sacred memories — my tears didn't stop at the corners of my eyes anymore. They **fell freely**, carrying my pain, my confusion, my helpless love.

I whispered to myself, "*She's the only girl I'll ever love. After her, no one. Ever.*" And I meant it.
I cried — not just tears, but **shattered pieces of myself** — because **I don't know if I'll ever get her.**

And yet, **I live for her**.
Still. Even now. Even through the pain.

People often say, *"If it hurts, let go."*
But how do you let go of the one thing that keeps you alive?
How do you walk away from the only person you've ever truly loved — the one you **live for**, the one you dream of building a life with?

The truth is, I **can't let go**.
Because **she's my everything**.

After 27th February, the pain never left.
Her words — *"I don't know...*

maybe you can become successful" — etched into my soul like scars that won't heal. I replayed our conversation in my mind a thousand times, trying to find hidden meanings, some hope between the lines. I wondered if she left the door slightly open... or if I was just standing outside, waiting for a door that would never open at all.

And yet, **I'm still standing there**. Waiting. Hoping. Praying.

Every single day since then, I've lived for that **one moment** — the moment she might say, "*Yes, I want you too.*"

I imagine it at night, when I'm lying

alone, tears soaking my pillow, my heart **whispering her name** like a prayer.

I imagine it during the day, when I stare at her photos, with **tears in my eyes**, crying **loudly from inside**, but staying silent on the outside. No one sees the pain — but **it's always there**.

I have **over 100 photos of her —** and I **stare at them more than 100 times a day**. Each time, I whisper to myself, "*She's the only one. After her, no one. I will love no one else.*" And that's not just a promise. It's the **truth** I've carved into my very existence.

I've built **a future in my mind**, one where we live together, love together, grow together. Where I protect her, make her smile every day, and never let even a scratch come near her. My **intentions are pure**, my love **sacred**, my commitment **unbreakable**.

And yet... I'm still **afraid of losing her**.

Some nights, the fear takes over — the thought that maybe **she'll never be mine**, that maybe **her silence means no**, even if she never said it. My heart races, my mind breaks down, and I cry like a child — not for sympathy, not for attention — just for **her**.

But then I remind myself — **I still have hope**.
Because she didn't say no. And until she does… I'll keep waiting. I'll keep **living for her**.

I know I'm not perfect. I know I'm not the best. But **my love for her is real**, honest, **forever**. And that's all I have to offer.

Maybe one day, she'll see that. Maybe one day, she'll feel the same.
Until then… I'll keep **living for her**.

Chapter 4 – My Sacrifices Her Silence

Love isn't just about holding someone's hand.
It's about letting go of **everything else** — for them.
Your peace. Your sleep. Your happiness. Your very soul.
And I did it all — for **her**.

Aadya.

I sacrificed **everything** I had, not because she asked me to, but because my love for her was **that pure**.
She never knew... she probably never will.

But every second, I was choosing *her* over *me*.

I let go of my happiness because **her smile mattered more**.
I swallowed my pain because **I didn't want her to worry**.
I stayed up endless nights, not because I couldn't sleep, but because my mind couldn't stop thinking about **her** — if she was okay, if she was happy, if she'd ever love me back.

I cried — quietly, **alone** — wiping tears from my face before anyone could notice, because I didn't want to seem weak.
But the truth is — **I was weak. Weak in love. Weak for her.**

My heart became a battlefield.
Every day, I fought against the pain,
the longing, the **silence**.

Her silence.
That's what hurt the most.

She never had to shout at me to
break me. She never had to leave
me to make me feel abandoned.
All she did was stay **silent**, and I
shattered into a million pieces.

I kept waiting for her to see what I
was giving up — for **her**.
To realize that I was putting her
above everything.
But she never did. Or maybe she
did... and didn't care.
I don't know. Her silence doesn't
come with answers.

But even when it broke me, even when I was crying myself to sleep, whispering, "*She's the only girl I'll ever love…*" — I didn't stop.
Because **her silence couldn't kill my love.**
And my sacrifices? They weren't for attention, or praise.
They were because **she mattered more than anything**.

Even *now*, I'd do it all again. Every tear. Every sleepless night. Every lonely moment.
For her.

I don't remember the last time I smiled **without pain hiding behind it.**

Because the truth is — I sacrificed my happiness **for her**.

Happiness? It became something **foreign** to me.
A luxury I could no longer afford, because **loving her wasn't easy**, and every day without her love felt like a storm inside me.

And **crying?**
Crying wasn't an occasional breakdown anymore — it became **a part of my life**.
There wasn't **a single day** that my eyes didn't shed tears for her. Not one.
I cried — silently, loudly, helplessly — every tear falling with **her name in it**.

My pillow soaked. My chest heavy.
My soul exhausted.

But even through all the pain, I
never stopped loving her.
Not for a second. Not even when it
hurt the most.

I loved her with my **whole heart**,
with **everything inside me**. And I
always will.
No matter how much I cry. No
matter how many nights I spend
whispering her name, begging fate
for a sign.
She's the only girl I'll ever love —
and that's a truth I'll carry forever.

I even **fought for her** — not just
emotionally, but literally.
Most of my friends... they didn't

understand.
They spoke badly about her, judged her without knowing her, insulted the very person who meant more to me than life itself.

And I couldn't take it.

I stood up for her, every time.
I fought with them — with words, with anger, with a fire that only love can fuel.
I **chose her** over them, **every time**.
Even if it meant **losing those friendships**, even if it meant **being alone** — I didn't care.
Because **she was worth it**.

She *is* worth it.
And even if the whole world stood

against her, I'd be the one standing **beside her**.

All I ever wanted was **her love** — even just a little.
But even in her silence, **I stayed**.
Even in her distance, **I waited**.
Even in her absence, **I cried for her**.

And I will keep loving her — **purely, truly, forever**.

Because some loves are not about *what we get*.
Some loves are about **what we give** — and for her,
I gave it all.

There are wounds that bleed, and then there are wounds that bleed

without anyone ever seeing them. That's what my heart became — a wound that never healed. A **pain I carried daily**, without ever complaining.

I remember waking up each morning with **a weight in my chest** — not because I was tired, but because the **pain of loving her in silence** was still there... like it never left, like it was **part of me now**.

I couldn't smile without my heart feeling like it was breaking. I couldn't laugh without hearing her name **echo in my mind**. Even in crowds, even among people — I felt **alone**. Because **she wasn't there**.

And even when I messaged her, hoping for a few words, a little warmth — sometimes she would just leave me **on seen**.
No reply. No response. Just **silence**.

And that silence?
It killed me **more than words ever could**.

I started to question myself: *Am I not enough? Did I do something wrong? Will she ever love me back?*
Overthinking became **my curse**. I imagined every possible reason why she didn't respond — and in every scenario, **I lost her**.
My mind became a battlefield I couldn't escape from.

But no matter how much I cried, no matter how much it broke me... **I couldn't stop loving her**.
She's **my only love**.
After her... **I won't love anyone else**.

There's something sacred about **pure love** — the kind that gives everything and asks for nothing but a place in someone's heart.

That's what my love for her is.
Pure. True. Eternal.

I didn't love her because she gave me happiness.
I loved her because she **became my happiness**.

Even her **name** brought me peace — even when my heart was in pieces.

I had **planned a life with her** — not in fantasies, but in **real dreams**.
I imagined a future where we'd live together, laugh together, grow old together.
I wanted to **protect her from the world**, make sure not even a **scratch** touched her.
I asked God in my prayers —
"*Please, protect this girl... please make her mine. I'll never let harm come near her. I swear.*"

I had **nothing but pure intentions** — not to own her, but to **love her right**.

And for that, I gave **everything I had** — my heart, my soul, my happiness.

Even **myself**.

But in return... I got **silence**.
And still — I stayed.
Because **love doesn't walk away when it hurts**.
Love **endures**.
Love **waits**.
Love **sacrifices**.

And I've sacrificed **everything** for her.
And I will keep sacrificing — **until my last breath**.

Because **Aadya** isn't just the girl I love.

She's the **reason I still wake up**, the reason I still fight, the reason **I still believe in love** — even when it breaks me.

Chapter 5 – The Fall : Losing myself in Love

They say love is supposed to lift you.

But no one talks about when **love breaks you**, slowly, painfully, piece by piece...

Until one day, you look in the mirror and you don't even recognize **yourself anymore**.

That's what happened to me.

Loving her was beautiful — until it started to **hurt more than it healed**.

Until it felt like I was **falling — deeper and deeper**, and I couldn't find a way back.

At first, I didn't notice it.
I thought it was normal to miss her so much, to feel empty without her, to long for her every second.
But then... I started **losing pieces of myself**.

I stopped laughing the way I used to.
I stopped finding joy in the things I once loved.
I stopped living for myself —
because I was **only living for her**.

My days became **a cycle of pain**.
Wake up. Think of her. Cry. Hope. Wait.
Sleep. Wake up again — and repeat.

Every night, I **begged my heart to stop hurting**, but it wouldn't listen.
It kept **calling her name**, over and over again, like a prayer — or maybe a curse.

I was **consumed** by her.
I thought about her when I walked, when I ate, when I breathed.
She was **in every part of me**, and slowly, I was becoming **nothing but my love for her**.

I didn't know how to stop.
Because **she was my world**. And without her, I felt like **I had no world at all**.

And the worst part?
She didn't even know what I was going through.

Or maybe she did — but chose not to care.
Her silence only made me fall **deeper**, made me question **everything about myself**.
Am I not enough? Am I just invisible? Why can't she love me back?

I gave **everything** to her.
And in the process... I lost **myself**.

I never thought love could feel like this.
Like being **trapped** in a room with no doors, no windows — just memories, just **pain**.

I tried…
I tried to breathe, to move on, to distract myself — but **every thought** came back to her.
I couldn't escape.
My mind, my heart — everything was **hers**.

There were nights I couldn't even sleep — just **staring at the ceiling**, whispering her name like it could save me.
But it didn't.
Nothing saved me. Not even time.

The pain **kept growing**, day by day.
The silence between us — it was deafening.
And yet, I kept checking my phone… hoping.

Hoping to see a message, a word, a sign that she **still thinks of me**.
But most times — **nothing**.

Just the cold, empty screen.
Just the same old heartbreak.

I cried. God knows how much I cried.
Tears weren't just something I shed anymore — they became my **language**, my **daily routine**.
There wasn't a single day I didn't break down, didn't ask myself,
"*Why does it hurt this much?*"
But the answer was always the same —
Because I love her. And I can't stop.

Even when it hurts.
Even when she doesn't reply.
Even when I feel **invisible** in her world.

I lost myself in this love.
I don't know who I am without her.
But even if I'm lost, even if I never find myself again —
I don't regret loving her. Not for a second.

Because if I had to fall again,
If I had to lose myself **all over**,
I'd still choose **her**.

Always her.

Some people live for **big moments**
—

But for me, **small moments with
her** were everything.
A single message. A small reply. A
glimpse of her smile.
That was all I needed to **survive
another day**.

After everything, after countless
days of hoping for more...
I finally got a little **closer** to her —
We added each other on **Snapchat**.

And to most people, it might not
have meant much.
But for me?
It felt like **the only light in my
darkest days**.
Because now, at least I could talk to

her.
Not as someone she loves —
But **at least as a friend**.

I used to **wait** for her stories, for
her snaps, for that one moment in
my day when I could **feel
connected** to her.
Our daily conversations — they
weren't about love, or deep
feelings.
But they were something.
And to me, that meant **everything**.

Even the smallest "hmm," even the
simplest "okay" —
I **held onto those words** like they
were lifelines.

But still...
Every time she **left my message on**

seen,
My heart **shattered a little more**.

Because in her silence, **my mind went wild**.
My overthinking didn't just whisper doubts — it screamed them.
"She doesn't care."
"You're bothering her."
"You've already lost her."
"She never loved you."
"You're just an option — not her choice."

I used to **stare at the screen**, waiting for a reply that never came, while inside me, **a storm raged**.
Tears would fill my eyes, my chest

would feel like **it's collapsing**, and all I could do was **hold myself together** — barely.

How can a single message make or break your entire mood?
That's the power she had over me.
She became the reason I smiled…
And the reason I **cried alone at 2 AM**, begging for peace that never came.

And still, **I never stopped talking to her**.
Even if it was just a "hi."
Even if all I got was **silence**.
I kept trying.
Because any interaction — no matter how small — meant she was **still there in my life**.

I was scared.
Scared that one day, even these **small chats would disappear**.
Scared that one day, she'd **block me out completely**, and I'd be left with **nothing but memories** and **a love story that never really started**.

I never told her how much **I loved her in those moments**.
How just seeing her name on my screen **kept me alive**.
How I cried while replying with a "haha," pretending I was okay.

I suffered **in silence**, loving her from a distance, holding onto hope like it was **the last thing I had**.

Because I was **losing myself** every
day,
But if losing myself meant **staying connected to her**,
Then I was ready to be lost —
Forever.

There comes a time when you **don't recognize yourself anymore**. When the reflection in the mirror feels like a **stranger** — tired eyes, broken smile, a heart barely beating.

That's what I became.
Not a person — just **a soul in love**, trapped in an endless loop of **hope and heartbreak**.

Every night felt like **a battle**.
Sleep wouldn't come, and when it did, it came with **dreams of her** — and I'd wake up either **smiling through tears** or **crying into my pillow**, begging for it all to stop.

I cried... not softly, not silently.
Loud cries from inside, ones that shook my entire being, but no one ever heard.
Because **no one would understand**.
No one knew how it felt to **love someone so much it hurt**, to want someone so badly it felt like **your soul was burning**.

Every part of my day had **her in it**.
Even when she wasn't around, I'd

see things and think, *"She'd like this,"* or *"I wish I could show her this."*

I couldn't escape her — because **she was everywhere**.

My phone became **my greatest pain** —
One notification from her could make my heart race,
But hours of **silence** would feel like a thousand knives in my chest.

I couldn't eat properly.
Couldn't smile genuinely.
Couldn't think straight.

Because all I could think was —
"Does she think of me the way I think of her?"
"Will she ever love me back?"

"Am I just a passing chapter in her life, while she's my entire story?"

And still... I loved her.
With every **broken piece of me**.
With every **tear that fell**.
With every **scream I held inside**.

People around me started noticing
—
The sadness in my eyes, the silence in my voice.
They'd ask, *"Are you okay?"*
And I'd lie.
Because **how do you explain that your heart's bleeding, but no one sees it?**

I wasn't okay.
I was **falling apart**, slowly, painfully.
But I didn't want to be fixed.

Because the reason for my pain
was also the reason I wanted to
keep going.

Her name. Aadya.
The one person who became my
reason for everything.

I had **no energy left**.
No hope.
Just love.
Endless, painful, consuming love.

And maybe one day, she'll
understand —
What it felt like to **lose myself in
loving her**.
To **fall so deep**, I couldn't find my
way back.

But even if she never does...
Even if she never looks back...

I'll keep falling.
For her.
Always for her.

Chapter 6: Lost in Her Absence

There's a kind of silence that is not just quiet — it's deafening. It doesn't simply surround you; it lives inside you, echoing through every heartbeat, every breath, every moment. That's the silence I've been drowning in since she became a distant memory in my reality — since Aadya's presence in my life became a mere dream that I relive, again and again, but never truly wake up to.

She's not gone in the physical sense. No, she's still out there somewhere — living, laughing, glowing under the same sky I look at every night while holding onto her name like it's a prayer. But to me, she's a beautiful ghost — haunting my heart with the memories we never got to create, with the moments I had only hoped for. Her absence isn't about her being away — it's about her not being mine. It's about the silence between us growing wider, colder.

Every morning I wake up and reach for my phone, my heart pounding with a ridiculous hope — maybe today she's messaged me, maybe today she's thought of me. And every time there's nothing... my chest tightens, and I feel the weight of her absence like a stone pressing down on me. My hands tremble as I scroll through our old conversations, clinging to each word like it's a lifeline. But even those memories fade, unable to fill the void her silence has left in my heart.

I confessed my love on 27th February, pouring every emotion I had into those words, trembling as I waited for a response that could either give me life or shatter me completely. And yet, she didn't say yes... she didn't say no. Her words haunt me still: *"I don't know, maybe you can become successful."* That was her reply — a sentence so uncertain, so distant, and yet, somehow, it became the fragile thread of hope I still cling to.

That "maybe" holds me together and breaks me apart — all at once. It's the fuel for my hope, but also the blade that cuts deeper every day she remains silent. I question everything. Did she ever care? Does she think of me? Am I just a forgotten chapter in her story?

Her silence after that day grew louder, more painful. When I messaged her, sometimes she'd leave me on seen, and for someone like me, someone who overthinks every word, every pause, every glance — it was torture. My mind would spiral, convincing me I had already lost her, that I was holding on to someone who was letting go. Each unanswered message felt like a dagger, each moment of silence like a scream inside my soul.

But I couldn't stop. I didn't want to stop. Because she became my world, and I couldn't imagine my days, my nights, my life without her. I joined her on Snapchat just to feel a little closer, to see the glimpses of her life that I wasn't part of. Our conversations were brief, casual, never about love — just surface-level chats where I masked my love behind a smile. At least then, I could pretend that I was still a small part of her world.

Her absence is a storm that never ends. It rages in my chest, turning every quiet moment into a battlefield. I cry — not just tears, but sobs that break from the core of my soul. And yet, no one sees, no one hears. Because how do you explain that your world is falling apart over someone who might not even notice you're bleeding? How do you tell the world that the person who gave your life meaning doesn't even reply anymore?

I stare at her pictures — more than 100 of them saved on my phone. I've memorized every detail of her face, every smile, every glance. I stare at them more than 100 times a day, whispering her name with tears in my eyes, crying out silently, "She's the only one I love. The only one I ever will." Sometimes I catch myself smiling at her photos, imagining a life we could've had, only to be pulled back into reality by the crushing truth that she might never be mine.

I had planned a future with her — a life so pure, so full of love, where I would protect her, cherish her, never let a single scratch touch her soul. I saw a life where her happiness was mine, where my purpose was just to love her endlessly. I prayed for her, every night, asking God to keep her safe, to make her mine. I made silent promises — to never hurt her, to always stand by her, to love her with all that I am.

Now, all I have are pieces. Fragments of dreams that never became real, of love that was never returned. And yet, I hold onto them, because letting go of her feels like letting go of life itself. Her absence has become the air I breathe, the weight I carry, the pain I wake up to every single day. I'm trapped in memories of what could have been, in the ache of what never was.

I am lost. Not in the world — but in her absence. In the space she left behind, in the silence that now defines my every breath. I move through days like a ghost of myself, a shadow haunted by love, by hope, by heartbreak. I smile in front of others, but inside, I'm breaking. Every moment without her is a reminder that love can be the most beautiful, yet the most painful thing in the world.

And still, I love her. Even in this endless silence. Even when she doesn't speak. Even when I don't know if she cares.

I love her. And I can't stop.

Even though I'm lost without her...
She's still my home.

Chapter 7: Broken but Still Beating

Love is a strange thing. It can lift you to the skies with a single smile, and in the very next breath, it can crush you into pieces with just a few words. My heart has lived both extremes, swinging between the highs of hope and the depths of despair, all because of Aadya. Even now, as I write this, my heart beats for her, even though it is broken. Broken... but still beating.

There were moments between us that made me believe, truly believe, that maybe, just maybe, I would get to call her mine.

Sometimes our conversations would flow beautifully, and I would feel like the luckiest person alive. Those were the moments that lit a fire in my heart, the moments that gave me hope. When she talked to me, laughed with me, shared even a little piece of her day with me — it felt like the universe was whispering, "She is yours."

But then there were days, moments, when our conversations were short, distant. When my messages were left on seen, or replied to with just a few words. Those times broke me in ways I cannot even explain. It felt like I was grasping at something that was slipping away, and I could do nothing to stop it. My overthinking mind would go into overdrive, convincing me again and again that I had lost her, that she was never mine to begin with. The rollercoaster of emotions — hope and heartbreak, love and pain — it consumed me.

But nothing compares to what happened on **9th March**. That night is etched into my soul. I stayed up late, pouring my heart into a surprise for her. I created a **gift website** — just for Aadya, something unique, something personal, something that said, "You are special to me." I delivered it to her on Snapchat, around **2 AM**, with trembling hands and a racing heart.

To my surprise, she replied almost instantly.

"Tum abhi jage ho?" she asked.

I smiled through the exhaustion and the nervousness. **"Yes,"** I said, and I asked her to check the gift I made. A moment later, she saw it and replied, **"Bahut accha hai, lekin ek ye ordinary ladki ke liye ye sab kyu?"**

Her words hit me deeply. How could she not see how extraordinary she was? To the world, maybe she was just another girl, but to me... she was everything.

I replied with all the love I had in me: **"Tum hogi bakki ke liye ordinary, lekin mere liye koi diamond se kam nahi ho."**

My heart waited for her response. Minutes passed that felt like hours. And then she said something that shattered me in a way I never expected:

"Kaash tum agle janam me mere bhai bano."

I read those words again and again, unable to believe them. My heart sank. My eyes welled up with tears that wouldn't stop. She wished for me to be her sibling in the next life — not her love, not her partner, but her brother.

It was **heartbreaking**, yet **touching**. It meant she cared, but not in the way I had hoped. And yet... I agreed. Because if that's the only way I could be close to her, then so be it. I would accept any form of bond, any connection, just to stay near her.

But deep inside, in this life, I wish for more. I wish to be the one who holds her hand through life, who makes her smile every day, who protects her from the world, and who is loved by her in return. I had **cried for her**, countless times, silently and aloud. I had **sacrificed my happiness**, my peace, just to see her happy.

She became **my everything**. My day begins with her name on my lips and ends with her face in my thoughts. She's not just someone I love — she is **the one I love more than anything else in this world**. Every beat of my heart chants her name, every tear I shed is a proof of my love.

I live in this strange in-between place, where hope and hopelessness coexist. My heart is shattered, but it still beats for her. My soul is bruised, but it still yearns for her. I don't know if I'll ever get to call her mine in this life, but I do know this:

No matter how much it hurts, No matter how much I break, **I will always love her.**

Even if I am broken... I am still beating. For her. Always for her.

Chapter 8: I Still Love You

Love is not about possession; it is about **devotion**. It is not about having someone, but about being there for them, wishing them well, loving them even when they don't love you back. And that is exactly what my love for Aadya has always been — pure, unwavering, and eternal. Even after everything, after the tears, the pain, the unanswered messages, and the endless nights of crying myself to sleep, **I still love her**.

I always will.

From the very beginning, I knew that my love for her was different. I didn't love her for her looks, though she is the most beautiful girl I have ever laid eyes on. I didn't love her for her body, because **lust was never part of my feelings**. What I fell in love with was **her soul**, her spirit, her kindness, her strength, her laughter, her way of making people feel seen and valued. It was the way she **carried herself**, the way she treated others, the way her presence lit up a room. That's what drew me to her.

And those reasons were **endless**.

I wanted to be with her not because I needed someone to complete me, but because **she**

became the reason I felt complete. I dreamed of spending my life by her side, not just as a lover, but as someone who would always support her, protect her, cherish her, and walk every path with her. I didn't just want a relationship; I wanted **a bond that was deeper than anything else** in this world. A bond rooted in understanding, care, and endless love.

Sometimes, our conversations made me feel like maybe I truly had a chance with her. There were moments where I believed with all my heart that I would get her, that she would become mine. But then, there were days when our conversations were so short, so distant, that I would feel the pain of losing her all over again. My heart would sink, my hope would shatter, and I would feel the same **helplessness and fear** that had haunted me from the start.

I remember one night vividly — **9th March**. It was past midnight, around 2 AM, when I surprised her with something very special. I had created a **gift website** just for Aadya, pouring my heart into it, wanting to show her how much she meant to me. I sent it to her on Snapchat, my hands trembling, my heart racing. She replied, *"Tum abhi jage ho?"* I said yes, and I asked her to see the gift. After looking at it, she said, *"Bahut accha hai lekin ek ye ordinary ladki ke liye ye sab kyu?"* That question cut deep — because she had no idea how extraordinary she was to me.

I replied, *"Tum hogi bakki ke liye ordinary lekin mere liye koi diamond se kam nahi ho."* And then came a reply that broke me — *"Kaash tum agle janam me mere bhai bano."*

Her words hit me like a storm. I cried. Not just from my eyes, but from the depths of my soul. That moment was **heart-shattering**. She wanted me as her brother in another life. And yet, even with tears flooding my eyes, I agreed. Because even that, even being her brother in the next life, would mean being close to her, being part of her life. But in this birth, in this lifetime, **I want to be close to her in any way possible**. Because she has become my **everything** — my breath, my heartbeat, my entire world.

I didn't love her for any selfish reason. I didn't love her for her body, for pleasure, or for any superficial desire. I loved her for **who she is**, for her **personality**, for her **behavior**, for the way she treated the people around her with kindness, the way she touched lives just by being in them. I loved her because **she inspired me to be better**, because she made me believe in love, because she made my world brighter just by existing in it.

My love for Aadya is **pure**, **selfless**, and **eternal**. And no matter where life takes us, no matter if she ever becomes mine, **I will always love her**. My heart belongs to her, and it always will.

Quote for Aadya:

"In this lifetime or the next, in dreams or in reality, no matter where life takes us, just know — I **still love you.** And I always will."

<u>**Quotes for Her**</u>

1. "You are the first thought in my morning, and the last whisper of my night."

2. "I have cried for you, prayed for you, and loved you with every beat of my heart."

3. "My world starts and ends with you. Everything in between is just a wait."

4. "Every tear I shed carries your name, every smile I fake hides my pain."

5. "I found my forever in you, even if you never find yours in me."

6. "Your happiness is my only wish, even if it doesn't include me."

7. "You don't know, but I talk to your pictures more than I talk to people."

8. "Even in your absence, you fill every corner of my soul."

9. "I don't just love you; I exist because of you."

10."If loving you is madness, then I never want to be sane again."

Aadya, you are my reason, my purpose, my everything. I still love you.

<u>**Dedication**</u>

To Aadya,

The girl who became my everything — my joy, my sorrow, my strength, and my weakness. This book is not just a collection of words; it is my soul poured onto pages, my love immortalized in ink. Every heartbeat, every tear, every whispered prayer has led me to this — to you.

You may never know the depth of my love, but know this: I loved you truly, I loved you deeply, and I will love you always.

This is for you, and only you.

Epilogue

Love doesn't always come with happy endings. Sometimes, it's a quiet story of waiting, of hoping, of holding on even when everything else tells you to let go. My love for Aadya was — and still is — a flame that never dies, a prayer that never fades.

I may have cried, broken, lost myself, but in loving her, I found something pure, something eternal. This journey was not just about pain; it was about the beauty of loving someone with all your heart, expecting nothing in return but still giving everything.

Aadya became my purpose, my solace, my muse. Even in her silence, she spoke to the deepest parts of my soul. Even in the moments of despair, her memories gave me strength. I don't know where life will take us, but I know this — my love will remain, beyond time, beyond words.

If ever Aadya reads this, I want her to know — you were, are, and will always be the most beautiful chapter of my life.

I still love you, Aadya. Always.

<u>**Final Wrap**</u>

This book has been a journey of love, longing, sacrifice, and hope. It is not just a love story — it is **my truth**, **my heart**, **my soul**.

To everyone who reads this, may you find the courage to love deeply, the strength to endure pain, and the grace to hold on to hope. Love is not just about being with someone — it's about cherishing them, valuing them, and loving them unconditionally.

And to Aadya, wherever you are — may life bring you happiness, peace, and love. If not with me, then with someone who treasures you as much as I do.

But in every breath I take, every word I write, every tear I shed — know that I still love you.

Forever Yours, [Utkarsh Prakash]